BASIC CHRISTIANITY
A NEW LIFE FORM

By: TOM S. HANSON

xulon
PRESS

Copyright © 2015 by Tom S. Hanson

BASIC CHRISTIANITY
A New Life Form
by Tom S. Hanson

Printed in the United States of America.

ISBN 9781498432191

All rights reserved solely by the author. The author guarantees all contents are original and do not infringe upon the legal rights of any other person or work. No part of this book may be reproduced in any form without the permission of the author. The views expressed in this book are not necessarily those of the publisher.

Unless otherwise indicated, Scripture quotations are taken from the New Living Translation (NLT). Copyright © 1996, 2004, 2007 by Tyndale House Foundation. Used by permission. All rights reserved.

Scripture quotations are taken from the New King James Version (NKJV). Copyright © 1979, 1980, 1982 by Thomas Nelson, Inc. Used by permission. All rights reserved.

Scripture quotations are taken from the New International Version (NIV). Copyright © 1973, 1978, 1984, 2011 by Biblica, Inc.™. Used by permission. All rights reserved.

www.xulonpress.com

6-2-2015

To: Mike

From: Tom S. Hansen

Thanks for all your help Mike.

A Dedication

I would like to express thanks to a number of people who continue to be meaningful in my life. They would be my wife, Kim, my older son, Mark and his wife Rikke and sons Z-man and Kai. Also thanks to my younger son, Matt and his fiancé, Beckie. Again thanks to my Tuesday morning Bible study group and my Thursday morning breakfast friends.

Special thanks to my sister, Twink, who will edit this book as she has done for my other books

INTRODUCTION

I have read quite a few books by different Christian writers who have proffered different concepts on the Bible. I usually have been impressed with their ability to discover different possibilities. After over 40 years and having participated in Charismatic, Pentecostal, and Evangelical fellowships; I now wonder at all the possibilities that have been put forth.

Because of this, I have decided to re-discover the original intent of the original authors. What was the message that Jesus and His disciples, through the Holy Spirit, were saying? What I have discovered is that Christianity is a new religion. It was not a continuation of the Old Testament. Even though there are many references to the Old Testament, The New Testament is its own separate religion.

As I studied it again and again, I came to realize that it was very different than the Jewish religion. Just as God chose to do a make over in The Old Testament with the Flood, God decided to have a "New Relationship" with His human creation by bringing forth "The New Faith" of Christianity.

After discovering that The New Testament represented a completely different "Faith" from that of the Old Testament, I began to explore to discover the reason why. To my surprise I discovered this happened many times in The Old Testament too. At that time humans also decided to speak for God in a way that enhanced their culture.

In the Old Testament we usually would see it happening when God would speak through His chosen prophet, at the time, to give a message to His people, the Jews. It was often a warning to His people that they needed to change the way they were doing things. If they did not change then He, God, would need to chastise them in some way.

Introduction

Over and over again we read how the people reacted. There were often quite a number of prophets and they were not the chosen prophets of God. They would not back up God's chosen prophet, such as Jeremiah, and they would prophesy good things. This normally would please the King and the people. Thus God's chosen prophet would not be listened to. The people and the king would rather hear good things. Thus they altered God's prophecy to enhance their own culture at the time.

It would seem that humans have been altering or changing God's Word for a long time in order to benefit their current situation. This bit of 411 (information) changed my opinion of what humans were doing and helped me to understand just how flawed we are in this area of our lives. As I continued to research this activity from the Old Testament to the New Testament, I discovered it was just humans being humans.

I would like to share a private event with you about what happened to me as I wrote this book. I was about

¾ of the way through when our Lord took me to "the woodshed". He let me know that even though I had discovered His original intent, I was presenting it with an Old Testament attitude. Because of this I had to begin the book anew.

This time it was with a New Testament attitude. You might ask what the difference was? My writing style was angry. I was taking out my anger in the way I wrote the book. God advised me that He was not angry over what I discovered. That is not the way God Rolls.

As you get into the chapter on "The Beatitudes", you begin to really understand God's Ethics. It's not that our Lord does not correct. He just corrects with an attitude of "Love". He first forgives our sins and then encourages us to try again with His style of "Love".

I was more than a little upset with what I discovered and was taking my anger out on those who have been altering our New Testament. I was allowing myself to be pushed by "good old" Old Testament anger. I sounded so righteous that I even impressed

Introduction

myself. Then our Lord graciously reminded me of how often He extended forgiveness and encouragement to "yours truly'.

Well as they say...the rest is history. I dumped my 1st attempt at revealing what I had discovered and went back to writing God's way. I pray that you will receive this 411 with "Love". And if you are moved to share this information, remember to share it with "Love".

Table of Contents

A Dedication v
Introduction vii
Book Premise xv

Chapter 1:   JESUS God the Son 23
Chapter 2:   The Relationship 30
Chapter 3:   Jesus Teaches God's Love 39
Chapter 4:   Let's Review 46
Chapter 5:   Paul & The Law 51
Chapter 6:   "Others Centered" 56
Chapter 7:   2nd Corinthians 5 63
Chapter 8:   A New Life Form 68
Chapter 9:   Christian Ethics In Action 75
Chapter 10: So What Am I Saying 85

Book Premise

The purpose of this book is to highlight an interpretation of The New Testament that has been overlooked for too long. Since Jesus and His chosen disciples introduced Christianity about 2000 years ago, it has not been uncommon for people to alter Christianity's "Relational" perspective to enhance their own cultures.

Perhaps the most interesting thing I have discovered in my search for the relevance of the New Testament is just how many people have altered it to enhance their particular culture and their humanity. Today we would call these alterations "interpretations". That is a long word, which means "an explanation of something that is not immediately obvious".

And of course we need to ask the question of "not obvious to whom"?

Today we know it can also just be an explanation to present an old idea in a new light. Also perhaps a method of explaining something in a different way in order to have it agree with what you want it to say. With a little theological slight of hand, we can have the Bible say just about whatever we want it to say. This last possibility is usually the method cultures have used to alter the obvious meaning of The New Testament in order to have The New Testament enhance their particular culture.

As I studied and prepped for this book, I realized we were doing the same thing in the good old USA as other cultures prior to ours did. Through <u>selective teaching</u> we have changed the message as it was originally intended to be.

I have been a Christian for over 43 years. I wish I could say that the opinion I'm expressing in this book is something I learned many years ago. I cannot do that. After many years of studying my Bible, I just

Book Premise

became aware of this interesting concept about 2 years ago. Now as I study The Old and New Testaments, I see it so clearly. I have included this last bit of 411 so that you, the reader, will realize my dilemma. I pass this 411 on to you and ask that you verify it in your own study.

Again, I had been a believer for over 40 years when I discovered what I have placed in this little book. Why is this fact important? A number of pastors I have listened to over the years have stressed the need to keep on searching the Bible for daily help. Having read The Old and New Testaments from cover to cover more than once, I thought I knew it all. Then their advice finally kicked in for me. Sometimes our Lord teaches us one thing in order to prepare us for the next thing.

An analogy would be like how schools require one course before we can take another course. Without the knowledge of one course, we will not be prepared to learn the stuff taught in the next course. When I was in school such was the case for math courses. 1st

it was basic math, then geometry and finally algebra & trig. The same is true in language courses.

Those of course are secular examples. In Christianity we need to be careful of the way we grow our faith. In the next few paragraphs I have used some pretty intense scriptures to make sure we do not stray from what our Lord says is acceptable. If you are not a believer I'm sure they would appear to be a little too narrow-minded.

Even believers might feel a little restrained by them. Just another reason why we need God The Holy Spirit to be our Mentor as He guides us into "Spiritual Maturity".

So let's take a look at some of those scriptures that will keep us learning as our Lord desires. The New Testament teaches that Jesus is the cornerstone of our "New Faith" of Christianity. Please turn in your Bible to 1st Corinthians & Chapter 3 & verses 10 & 11. The NKJ says; "(10) According to the grace of God which was given to me, as a wise master builder I have laid the foundation, and another builds on it. But let each one take heed how he builds on it. (11) For no other foundation can anyone lay than that which is laid, which is Jesus Christ." Paul lets us know in no uncertain terms that all Christian teaching must be built on the foundation that is Jesus Christ.

Perhaps the most known scripture that ties into the previous verses by Paul is found in the 7th chapter of Matthew's Gospel. Please turn in your Bible to Matthew 7:24, also in the NKJ; "Therefore whoever hears these sayings of Mine, and does them, I will liken him to a wise man who built his house on the rock." Verses 25 through 27 complete this story. Of course the rock is Jesus. Jesus is teaching through the method of analogy. The house in this example is our body. When we base our life on Jesus, who is our rock, we will be able to stand against all the storms of life. If we build our hopes on anything other than Jesus, the storms of life will overcome us

Sometimes we believers need to learn one thing from our Lord before He can teach us another. That is why I believe we need to continue to study our Bibles consistently. I believe that it is God The Holy Spirit, within us, that help's us to learn and apply the truths we discover as we consistently study our Bibles.

As you will read later on in this book, God is always "Others Centered". All that He teaches us in our Bibles is "Others Centered". God, through our Mentor The Holy Spirit, never uses shortcuts. Even if we might not understand all our Bibles tell us, we need to realize that God is right. Remember, He is The Creator and we are the created.

As you read through this little book I will challenge you to be aware that human believers have altered The New Testament to meet their needs. We need to understand that God is in the process of conforming us to the image of His Son, Jesus. It is not about us transforming The New Testament into a book that will allow us to achieve success in our humanity. We already have received all that we could possibly desire.

If forgiveness for sins and life ever after with our Lord is not enough, then perhaps you should choose a system of belief that lets you remain just a human.

CHAPTER 1

JESUS GOD THE SON

It would seem that some believers have a hard time understanding what happened about 2000 years ago. To many believers it would appear that some men, a rather interesting group led by someone named Jesus, came up with a continuation of The Old Testament that they named The New Testament. Because it involved the same main God and was 1st introduced in Israel to Jews, a number of believers then and today just considered it an add on that fit the times.

Upon a complete study of the whole New Testament, we discover that it is not just an extension of The Old Testament. Even as God caused the flood in Noah's time to start new, so He brought an end to the Old Testament and began Christianity. It does have references to the Old Testament, but it has its own requirements.

So, who is Jesus? Please open whatever Bible you have to John's Gospel and chapter 1. We will quote out of the NKJ (New King James) from John 1:1-5; "(1) In the beginning was the Word, and the Word was with God, and the Word was God. (2) He was in the beginning with God. (3) All things were made through Him, and without Him nothing was made that was made. (4) In Him was life, and the life was the light of men. (5) And the light shines in the darkness, and the darkness did not comprehend it."

Let's do a little commentary on these verses. One of the titles we know Jesus by is the "Word". From these verses we know that He, Jesus, is God. We also know that He seems to take the point on making things. It would also appear that He has taken the point on introducing and establishing the "New Faith" of Christianity. The change was a decision that God

(Father, Son & Holy Spirit) were all in agreement on. All 3 of the Trinity were on hand to accomplish this change in Their desire to have a relationship with Their creation.

What is the change we are looking at? God (Father, Son & Holy Spirit) decided to end the "religion" of the Old Testament in favor of the "Relationship" of The New Testament. Also, this "New Relationship" would be made available to everyone. No longer would God call only the Hebrews His children.

In the New Testament we discover the inclusion of <u>all humans</u> in God's plan for salvation. Jew and Gentile, Man and Woman, Slave and Free. The only requirement for the "Relationship" God now offers is found in John's Gospel in verse 3:16. The NKJ says it this way: "For God so loved the world that He gave His only begotten Son, that whoever believes in Him should not perish but have everlasting life."

I know this verse sounds very simplistic. In order to fully understand what it means is one of the reasons we need to have a good understanding of this

"New Faith" we call Christianity. We also need to have a good handle on the word "believe" used in the previous scripture verse.

The dictionary has several definitions for the word believe. They run the gamut of accepting or taking something to be true to basing your life on a stated fact. I know we all want eternal life, but do we really believe that this verse qualifies us for eternal life?

For my wife and I, we heard the "Good News" and wanted to believe it. At first we were delighted with what had happened. But soon some doubts began to creep in. I mean really, how could such a thing be true? So what did we do?

We began to study our Bible in order to understand why it was true. We discovered in the book of Ephesians by the Apostle Paul in the 1st chapter that it was God The Holy Spirit that helped us to believe that what had happened was true. We both agreed that in our inner most soul that we felt this was true.

At the time I was traveling quite a bit for the corporation I was working for. Most of the business people

I worked with and was in contact with were definitely at odds with my "born again" Christian experience.

I bought my 1st surfboard in 1959 and in the business community this in itself was a no...no. Then I added the beginning of a new Christian life to this and my associates in the business world did not quite know what to think of me. Fortunately I was a success at business and for the most part they accepted me.

As the years went by, we continued to study our Bible and attend church and Bible studies under Chuck Smith and his Calvary Chapel.

This was when Calvary Chapel was on Sunflower & Greenville in Costa Mesa in 1971 during the middle of "The Jesus Movement". Then came one large tent and a 2nd large tent a block over on Fairview and Sunflower. After a while all the members pitched in and we built a new sanctuary. It was and is a very beautiful church, but I do confess I miss the little one on Sunflower & Greenville.

During this time we made some great friendships with other believers and grew to know our Lord more and more.

Chuck Smith was a great pastor. He would take us through the whole Bible every 2 years. He would do this through sermons on Sunday and verse by verse teaching at Bible studies during the week. As our Biblical knowledge increased year after year, so did our belief in our salvation.

God The Holy Spirit increased our confidence in the decision my wife and I had made over the years. Now, as we learn more and more about our faith, our confidence continues to grow.

This was the path my wife and I took to further our belief in the salvation we had been offered. So, what path did you take to finally come to an understanding and confidence of the word "believe" in your life?

During these years I believe that God knew it was necessary to help us receive the type of love He specializes in. The assurance of His love for me helped me to trust Him. We must always be able to receive His "Agape" love to learn just how much He loves us.

As you continue to read on in this little book, you will discover that God's Agape style of love is completely "Others Centered". In other words, His style of love is based solely on our need.

I pray that you don't mind that I have placed a little personal knowledge in this 1st chapter. My prayer is that it might help you to contemplate your relationship with our Lord.

Now that we, with Biblical assurance, have established that Jesus is God, let's move on.

We have now arrived at the point in this story where Jesus and His selected disciples begin the task of introducing this "New Faith" of Christianity. In the next chapter we will begin demonstrating the technique they would use to help their intended new believers accept this "New Faith".

CHAPTER 2

THE RELATIONSHIP

In the previous chapter we talked about the beginning of the "New Faith" of Christianity. Now lets take a look at how God brings this all about.

If we were to study our Bibles in order to learn how Jesus wants His new believers to represent Him we should look at "The Sermon On The Mount" which is found in Matthew 5:1-12. This is at the very beginning of the introduction of Christianity. Jesus is teaching His disciples and a large crowd the values He cares about. In the NLT (New Living Translation) it says; "(3) God blesses those who are poor and realize their need for him, for the Kingdom of Heaven is theirs. (poor in this situation speaks not to money, but to a person's moral worth) (4) God blesses those who mourn, for they will be comforted. (mourn in this situation is about lack of moral values in themselves and those around them) (5) God blesses those who are humble, for they will inherit the whole earth. (This verse is about "others centered" rather than self-centeredness) (6) God blesses those who hunger and thirst for justice, for they will be satisfied. (justice in this verse refers to moral justice) (7) God blesses those who are merciful, for they will be shown mercy. (this is the ability to feel leniency and compassion towards people who perhaps themselves live in a self-centered manner) (8) God blesses those whose hearts are pure, for they will see God. (they will see God because their hearts agree with God's heart) (9) God blesses those who work for peace, for they will be called the children of God. (because they live a God like life that seeks peace for all) (10) God blesses those who are persecuted for doing right, for the Kingdom of Heaven is theirs. (they do the right & compassionate thing because it is the same action

God would take) (11) God blesses you when people mock you and persecute you and lie about you and say all sorts of evil things against you because you are my followers. (these are people who are more concerned about God's heart rather than man's heart)

(12) Be happy about it! Be very glad! For a great reward awaits you in heaven. And remember, the ancient prophets were persecuted in the same way. (These are people who care more about God's ways than man's ways)

We know these scriptures as "The Beatitudes". I have taken the liberty of placing in brackets comments on each of these scriptures to help us understand their application. Jesus defined the "New Faith" of Christianity with these moral values. It is important to note that all of His disciples were there with the multitude to hear these values. Also, in all the Gospels and books to follow, it is these values that are taught over and over again.

I have a friend in Hawaii, named Ivan, who asked me about Christian ethics one day. I believe these verses we know as "The Beatitudes" define the Christian ethics and the "New Faith" Jesus came to introduce.

In the following chapters we will examine "Christian Ethics" and how different they are from the ethics we humans normally pattern our lives after. It's not that we humans are not capable of Godly morals, it's just that we are more capable of looking out for number 1.

It gets back to the difference between being self-centered and "Others Centered". Also, we humans have a bad habit of judging another's motives rather than questioning our own motives. The Bible speaks very pointedly to this activity. Check out in your Bible in the Gospel of Matthew 7:1-2; "(1) Judge not, that you be not judged. (2) For with what judgment you judge, you will be judged; and with the measure you use, it will be measured back to you." This quote is from the NKJ.

Why do you think Jesus would say such a thing? It is perhaps the core of whom we are representing in this life. Christianity asked that we represent Jesus to all we are involved with every day. It apparently does not matter what the other person has said or done. The

Bible says that we are not to judge them. In fact, it says that as we judge we will be judged. Is that what we want? I don't think so. As God loves and forgives us, so we get to love and forgive them.

Check out in your Bible Matthew 5:39-42. The NLT says; "(39) But do not resist an evil person! If someone slaps you on the right cheek, offer the other cheek also. (40) If you are sued in court and your shirt is taken from you, give your coat, too. (41) If a soldier demands that you carry his gear for a mile, carry it two miles. (42) Give to those who ask, and don't turn away from those who want to borrow."

!!! Really !!!

Is this what we signed up for? I'm not messing with you friends; this is straight out of The New Testament and is part of what "Christian Ethics" are all about.

MacDonald, in his "Believer's Bible Commentary", says; "Our obsession with material goods and possessions makes us recoil at the thought of giving away what we have acquired. However, if we were willing to concentrate on the treasures of heaven and be content with only necessary food and clothing, we would accept these words literally and willingly."

!!! **<u>RIGHT</u>** !!!

I don't know about you, but that was a rough one for me. I mean after all; are we just supposed to be some kind of "milk toast" or "wimp"? No wonder many Christians decide to include some of The Old Testament in their New Testament lifestyle. You know, a little "eye for an eye" or "tooth for a tooth". Some of those good old verses back in the Old Testament that are part of the "law".

Turn in your Bible to Matthew 5:43-48. The NKJ says it this way; "(43) You have heard that it was said, You shall love your neighbor and hate your enemy. (44) But I say to you, love your enemies, bless those who curse you, do good to those who hate you, and pray for those who spitefully use you and persecute you, (45) that you may be sons of your Father in heaven; for He makes His sun rise on the evil and the good, and sends rain on the just and the unjust. (46) For if you love those who love you, what reward have you? Do not even the tax collectors do the same? (47) And if you greet your brethren only, what do you do more than others? Do not even the tax collectors do so? (48) Therefore you shall be perfect, just as your Father in heaven is perfect." To help us really understand these verses we need to know that Jewish tax collectors were hated. They often collected more taxes than required and kept it for them selves. They did this to their own people.

WHO DOES GOD EXPECT US TO BE ?

Or, how about some more in Matthew 7:3-5. This is in regards to blaming others and is from the NLT; "(3) And why do you look at the speck in your brother's eye, but do not consider the plank in your own eye? (4) Or how can you say to your brother, let me remove the speck from your eye; and look, a plank is in your own eye? (5) Hypocrite! First remove the plank from your own eye, and then you will see clearly to remove the speck from your brother's eye."

!!! ENOUGH !!!

All of these verses from the 7th chapter of Matthew speak to our human proclivity (a natural inclination) to see another person's problem without 1st seeing and dealing with our own problems. Also, these verses help us to more clearly see the problem within us of being self-centered.

Do you see the problem? Verses like these truly help us to understand the difference between God's Ethics and the ethics of humans. God understands that this is the natural feeling of humans. As I mention in the last paragraph of this chapter, God deals directly with this human problem.

As we read through the New Testament we observe Jesus and His chosen Apostles both speaking these "ethics" and living them. These are the "ethics" The

New Testament is based on. The local people of that day seemed to enjoy that "Relational" approach as compared to the typical Old Testament approach as practiced by the Pharisee's and Sadducee's.

They, the locals, also enjoyed the forgiveness examples our Lord and His Apostles extended to them. For perhaps the 1st time they were able to feel the "Love" that God had for them.

And of course we will closely examine the special help God gives to those who choose His loving offer. These will be the verses that talk about God placing God The Holy Spirit into each believer at the time of their salvation. He is the One who will help us in our desire to be "Others Centered".

This is that special help I mentioned earlier in this chapter. God not only shares His ethical values with us; He also, with a part of Himself within us, helps us to have His Ability to live these values.

CHAPTER 3

JESUS TEACHES GOD'S LOVE

When we study the New Testament we learn our Lord's desire for how He wants us to live. In this chapter we will look at some more verses that Jesus spoke and modeled. Remember, He came to Earth as a combination of God and human. Thus He was tempted by many of the same temptations that you and I face everyday. The difference is that His God part was able to overcome the temptations that our human part sometimes gives into.

I used to think how unfair that was. Of course He could overcome His human desires, because of His

God part. I mean really; if I was part God then I would also be able to overcome my human temptations.

Then as I continued to study the New Testament, I discovered the fact that all Christians are part human and part Spirit. Remember those verses in Ephesians where the Apostle Paul tells us that all believers receive God The Holy Spirit within them at the time of salvation. Also, in 1st Corinthians 2:10-12, where Paul tells us why God has given us His Holy Spirit. Among other things, this allows us to know the mind of God. So what's the problem? Why is it so hard to change?

It's hard to change because we humans continue to try to change with our own inability. One of the many awesome changes Jesus introduced in The New Testament was the gift of God The Holy Spirit within the believer. I think this is why we experience God forgiving us and encouraging us. If we ask for His help, He will help us with His Ability.

Along with the verses I mentioned earlier in this chapter that prove we have received this special gift are some other interesting verses in John's Gospel. We know in John's Gospel that Jesus tells His disciples that He will send them God The Holy Spirit to live within them when He goes back to the Father. Jesus knows they will need this special "Helper".

Let's take another look at those verses in John's Gospel that talk about Jesus sending The Holy Spirit to live within His disciples after He goes back to Heaven. I will not quote the verses directly, but will display them in bullet form.

John 14:16 He will be our advocate and never leave us.

John 14:17 He leads us into all truth.

John 14:26 He will teach us and remind us of everything Jesus has told us.

John 15:26 He will testify all about Jesus.

John 16:7 If Jesus does not go back to Heaven, the Holy Spirit will not come.

Jesus said these things to His disciples prior to His crucifixion. He knew they would need this help when He was not there in person to help them. The key question we need to ask and answer is whether or not all of His followers to come later would also receive this special gift. Obviously I believe this special gift has been given to all of us who believe.

In my last book, **The Path To Spiritual Maturity**, I wrote about this situation. Some of my proof verses I wrote about in that book are found in the 3rd chapter of John's Gospel. In verses 1-7 is recorded the conversation between Jesus and Nicodemus. This is where Jesus reveals to Nicodemus the assurance His believers will have that they will join Him in Heaven. That assurance is none other than God The Holy Spirit living within the believer.

I find it very interesting how many believers in the USA have been convinced that because we have the completion of the Bible that we no longer need the Holy Spirit. What about what Jesus said to Nicodemus about God The Holy Spirit being required for entrance to Heaven?

To start with, do we really believe that it is our completed Bible that gets us into Heaven? (Give me a break) I don't remember this as being part of John 3:16.

So why have I brought all this up in this chapter? The title of this chapter has to do with God's style of love.

As I have mentioned before, the chief motivating factor in God's style of love is the ability to be "Others Centered" rather than being self- centered. After spending quite a bit of time studying The Old Testament, I've come to realize that this human problem has been around since creation. So, what can we do about it?

One of the many wonderful things about The New Testament and the "New Faith" of Christianity is how

God (Father, Son, & Holy Spirit) chose to give us a leg up on following His desires.

Along with awesome changes like forgiveness of sin, guarantee of our personal trip to Heaven, is the inclusion of a part of God placed within us. Why would God do such a thing? I believe the answer lies within our human inability to be "Others Centered".

Throughout our lives, some more and some less, we have a problem of dealing with things that tempt us to be more self-centered than "Others Centered". God, being the thoughtful creator that He is, decided to bless us with this gift of God The Holy Spirit when we became Christians. God's help in this matter is not automatic. We need to seek the help of God The Holy Spirit to help us make "Others Centered" choices.

Many Pentecostal and Charismatic Christians believe in the indwelling of God The Holy Spirit. Unfortunately many tend to think this gift from God is for their benefit to use on themselves. I do believe in specific gifts for certain individuals. This book is about the gift from The Holy Spirit that is for all believers to give us God's Ability to represent Him.

Many Evangelical Christians do not believe in the indwelling of God The Holy Spirit. Because many Evangelicals reject the indwelling I am talking about, they also reject the help that God The Holy Spirit was designed to give human believers. It turns out that this gift from God is to enable us in our effort to be more "Others Centered" and less self-centered.

As we look at real life examples of Jesus applying this "Others Centered" ability, we will realize and appreciate His helping us in also becoming "Others Centered" and not being so self-centered. Also, we will understand that without His help we, as normal humans, cannot be the reps God is looking for us to be.

In the "New Faith" of Christianity, it's all about those who God has chosen to accept the help He has provided us. Aside from helping us "Roll" as God "Rolls", He, God The Holy Spirit, helps us to receive the "Love" God has for us. That "Love" includes both forgiveness and encouragement.

CHAPTER 4

LET'S REVIEW

I know that the 1st 3 chapters might be a little hard for you to ingest. I pray that along with some of the discoveries God has allowed me to see that you will take the time to study for yourself the Bible verses I have included.

For a number of years I have enjoyed studying some Christian history of how cultures were changed by it and in turn changed it to help them selves.

As I mention in another chapter, these alterations tend to be a typical human reaction. Humans just seem to be wired to be in control of their own lives. This seems especially true in the good old USA.

Let's Review

Unfortunately this human tendency to be in control clashes with the theory I have discovered. It is that in the "New Faith" of Christianity it is God who is in control. When we accept His unbelievable offer of salvation, we are no longer who we used to be. I think this is probably the main reason we become types of "Judiazers".

This group was an offspring from some of those 1st believers in Jerusalem. All of the 1st believers were Jewish and from the Jerusalem area and some other parts of Judea. They believed in the salvation from Jesus, but also kept some aspects of The Old Testament law that they believed would make them better Christians. In other words they wanted some control in their lives and by obeying certain areas of the Mosaic Law, they were helping to earn their salvation.

By becoming a type of "Judiazer", it allows us to somehow, in our own power, to earn the things that God desires to give us for free.

Do you begin to see the elephant in the room as relates to being a type of "Judiazer"? The whole "New Faith" of Christianity is about God giving His gift freely. It is never about us humans earning that gift.

Unfortunately, humans seem to be wired to have a hard time accepting something for free. Humans tend to want to somehow, in their own power, earn it. I think this is the reason that we adopt a tad of a "Judiazer" role. By not only accepting God's salvation, but also including obeying certain "laws" in The Old Testament, we can feel as though we are earning it.

I have spent a little time in this chapter on our proclivity toward becoming Judiazers. And remember the word proclivity means to have the propensity to be a certain way. One of the reasons is to prepare you for the next chapter where the Apostle Paul deals directly with some of the original Judiazers who have attacked his credibility as the Apostle to the Gentiles and his preaching this Gospel to the Galatians.

Let's Review

As long as we fall back on our own inability instead of relying on God's Ability, we will miss the point of 2nd Corinthians 5:17 and the role God is allowing us to fulfill.

In our own ability we continue to use God for our own greed, rather than allow God to use us for His purpose. That is why so often we tend to be concerned more for what we deem as necessary to live this life rather than living this life for God.

Our humanness is very important to us. Because of that, we have a hard time realizing the fact that we are no longer who we use to be. God's offer of salvation caused who we use to be to die and allowed us to be "born again". The Christian Ethics I write about in this book are written in our New Testament to those who have been "born again".

So I pray that you are following the Christian life I am presenting so far. Again, as I relate later in this book, I have been a believer for over 40 years. I did not discover the 411 I am presenting in this little book at the beginning. Please consider the different scriptures I am using to track with me.

In the next chapter we will further discover the Apostle Paul that Jesus appointed to be the Apostle to the Gentiles.

See you there.

CHAPTER 5
PAUL & THE LAW

The Apostle Paul was the last Apostle we read about in the New Testament. The story of his conversion to Christianity is very interesting. It begins in the book of Acts in chapter 7 after Stephen has delivered his indictment against the Pharisees. At this time Paul is known as Saul. He is a Pharisee and against the "New Faith" of Christianity. The story picks up again in chapter 9 of Acts. This is when Saul is on the road to Damascus and our Lord interrupts his trip in a rather dramatic fashion.

I'll let you finish that story on your own. The bottom line is that Jesus chose Saul to be His Apostle to the Gentiles and renamed him Paul. Jesus also taught Paul in person after He had been crucified and went back to Heaven.

Please turn with me in your Bible to the book of Galatians. Paul had successfully introduced these people to Jesus. Later however, they, the Galatians were visited by certain Christians from Jerusalem who had altered the message of Jesus. They believed that Jesus was necessary for salvation but it was also necessary to obey "the law" to perfect your faith.

The Apostle Paul answers this problem in chapter 2 of Galatians in verses 15-16. The NLT says it this way as he explains to the Galatians using an example of the Apostle Peter; "(15) You and I are Jews by birth, not sinners like the Gentiles. (16) Yet we know that a person is made right with God by faith in Jesus Christ, not by obeying the law. And we have believed in Christ Jesus, so that we may be right with God because of our faith in Christ, not because we have obeyed the law. For no one will ever be made right with God by obeying the law."

Let's do a little commentary on these verses. Paul was more than a little ticked off at this situation. He, Paul, had personally been appointed the Apostle to the Gentiles by Jesus.

We find this 411 in Galatians chapter 1. I think these verses in Galatians definitely dot the "i" and cross the "t" on the question of Christians needing to obey the letter of the "law" as defined in the Old Testament.

Many believers today seem to have adopted some of the customs of these people that Paul was referring to. Today we know them as Judiazers. They have altered the true "New Faith" as introduced by Jesus Christ, by adding aspects of the Old Testament's letter of the "law".

In Galatians 1:8-9 Paul lets the new Galatian believers completely understand the Christian position on adding to what Jesus has said. In the NLT we read; "(8) Let God's curse fall on anyone, including us or even and angel from heaven, who preaches a different kind of Good News than the one we preached to you. (9) I say again what we have said before: If anyone preaches any other Good News than the one you welcomed, let that person be cursed." I think the above scriptures by the Apostle Paul are quite clear. Don't add or subtract from God's word.

There is a similar verse back in Proverbs 30:6 that states in the NKJ; "Do not add to His words, Lest He rebuke you, and you be found a liar."

Unfortunately we humans seem quite at home altering things to make them better for us. Altering the Bible in both The Old Testament and in The New Testament just seems to happen by humans who want to improve on it. Guess what? These types of alterations are not an improvement.

I find the Apostle Paul an interesting choice by our Lord. First of all he was a Jew. He was born outside of Israel, but was schooled by none other than one of the highest ranking Pharisees, Gamaliel.

Because of his father being Jewish, he inherited Roman citizenship. Because of his birth and younger years in Tarsus, he was knowledgeable on the Greek society. So here we have a man steeped in Old Testament knowledge and also adept at interacting with Gentiles.

What a great combination to be chosen by our Lord as the Apostle to the Gentiles. His combination of Old Testament knowledge and knowing about Gentiles made him the perfect choice to further the "New Faith" of Christianity.

AGAIN, WHO CREATED WHOM?

CHAPTER 6

"Others Centered"

Unfortunately the word we are most familiar with in regards to the heading of this chapter would be self-centered. The trait of being self-centered is very common in humans. We have a number of funny ways to describe this condition. My favorite is when this condition is prevalent in one of my friends. We wave a hand above our heads in a circle and claim "its all about me".

If this condition were not so prevalent in humans, it would be humorous. Unfortunately, that is the way we usually roll in our relations with other humans and even our God.

Fortunately this is not the way God Rolls. His way of Rolling is the opposite of "It's all about me". Thus His way is always "Others Centered". Go back to the chapter on "The Beatitudes" and re-read them. They are all "Others Centered".

Perhaps one of the greatest characteristics of Christianity is that our God knows our inability to be this. He has witnessed for way too long how His creation tends to be self-centered.

I have studied the New Testament and the introduction of the "New Faith" of Christianity for many years. Perhaps the most consistent teaching of Christianity is its dedication to "Others Centeredness". Every Gospel and Epistle has this trait as there focus.

When I became a believer in 1971, during "The Jesus Movement", Chuck Smith and his Calvary Chapel introduced me to Jesus and His desire that we represent Him by also being "Others Centered". It was very refreshing to be a part of the Love our Lord has for His creation of humans.

Even with that focus humans, who have found salvation through Jesus, seem to be looking for ways to return to a life of "self-centeredness". They alter the words of The New Testament in order to try to make it support their sinful desires. To accomplish this sinful act they take verses out of context and add back parts of the Old Testament. Before you knew it, the focus is back on the individual instead of the "Others Centeredness" of Jesus.

I have studied this situation for a while now. My answer may or may not surprise you. We humans, as I have said before in prior chapters, just have a hard time not being in control. We are so much this way that we have, somehow, come up with a theory that "**IT IS**" all about us.

We do allow God to be responsible for getting us to Heaven and we do accept the death of Jesus on the cross as payment for our sins; past – present – and future. Unfortunately, we just don't know our Bibles well enough to understand them in the context they were written to us.

We seem to combine scriptures willy-nilly in order to have them say what we want them to say. The dictionary defines the term willy-nilly as in a random manner. Words like, every which way, haphazardly, indiscriminately and my favorite…arbitrarily. Of course I asked myself how this could happen. I mean, when I study my New Testament now it seems quite clear.

Then I realized the problem. The "New Faith" of Christianity is about humans obeying God and not God being there to help humans when they need Him. Sorry about this truth. There are times in my own life when I also wish He functioned like my self-centered nature would like.

There is a verse in Romans 8:28 that is a good example of how we alter God's word to fit our own needs. In the NLT it says; "And we know that God causes everything to work together for the good for those who love God and are called according to his purpose for them."

Many Pastors, Priests, and Ministers tend to teach this verse to let us know that God has our backs to help us when we need help. Do any of you see the "elephant" in the room yet? This verse is quite definite on whose purpose it is. It is God's purpose and not our purpose.

Check out the next verse, Romans 8:29, to discover the context of Romans 8:28. "For God knew his people in advance, and he chose them to become like his Son, so that his Son would be the firstborn among many brothers and sisters". We need to remember that we, God's creation, do not control God. God, our creator, controls us. If we continue on with verses 30-39 we discover that this is a good thing. It is a good thing as long as we believe what God says about it.

Again, this is just one example among many of how we humans try to control God. We alter the context of His word so that we can feel like we are in control.

Once God has chosen us, He begins to shape us into the image of His Son. Again, refer to the above verses in Romans chapter 8. Some times this can hurt a bit.

"Others Centered"

I have had talks with God when His shaping is not very fun for me. He is always right; it just does not always feel good to be conformed to the image of Jesus. I tend to think God should help me according to my human self-centered purpose, but that is not His purpose. Remember, it is about us being conformed to the image of Jesus.

It is not about God being like a Santa Claus to meet our greed. When we make God a Santa Claus figure we are trying to take control. We want it to be all good from our perspective. God promises to make it all good from His perspective. That usually requires some changes on our part that may or may not be pleasant.

Just to make sure we are on the same page here, let me list a few examples that yours truly has asked God for. For much of my life I have been overweight. I have asked God many times to help me lose some extra weight. I usually did not want this prayer, or wish, to involve any exercise or changes in my eating habits.

Also, more coin would solve many problems. Even though I was allowed to make quite a bit of coin in my business life, somehow it was never enough. I would ask God to increase my coin. Then I would get the feeling that perhaps my concern should not be about my desire for more coin, but that perhaps God desired that I would be more concerned with another's need for more coin. Yeah…right.

I can't tell you how many times I would get upset over another persons bad driving habits. This list could go on and on, but let's take a little pity on yours truly. I mean really; who enjoys looking back over their own self-centeredness?

The good news is that now I don't ask God to help my desire to enhance my life. Well…a lot less than I used to. After all, it is a journey and thank God He doesn't require us to change all at once.

In the next chapter we will get into the meaning of life as we study 2nd Corinthians.

See you there!

CHAPTER 7

2ND CORINTHIANS 5

The 1st 9 verses of this chapter deal with the here and now and the then and there. In both situations there is one constant condition. The answer is what we find in verse 5 of chapter 5 of 2nd Corinthians. The NLT says; "(5) God himself has prepared us for this, and as a guarantee he has given us his Holy Spirit."

So God The Holy Spirit is in us while we are on earth helping us to be conformed to the image of Jesus. He then escorts us to heaven.

Why is this important? As I wrote in my last book, The Path To Spiritual Maturity, if we are a Christian, then we are a **"new life form"**. This bit of 411 is highlighted by Jesus when He talks to Nicodemus in the 3rd chapter of John's Gospel. The bottom line of that discussion is that only those who have received God The Holy Spirit within them will go to heaven. Those who have not, will not go to heaven.

In verses 10-16 of John's Gospel Jesus continues His conversation with Nicodemus explaining some of the basic facts about the "New Faith" of Christianity. Now let's get back to 2nd Corinthians.

What do we learn from 2nd Corinthians 5:17. This verse sums up the previous verses in this chapter. It says in the NLT; "(17) This means that anyone who belongs to Christ has become a new person. The old life is gone; a new life has begun!". The NKJ says the same verse this way; "(17) Therefore, if anyone is in Christ, he is a new creation; old things have passed away; behold, all things have become new".

Why are we a new creation? Before salvation we were 100% human. After salvation we became part human and part Spirit. Therefore we are not the same as we used to be. What then does the Bible say is our new responsibility?

Verse 18 through the end of chapter 5 answers that question. We become ambassadors for God to those who have still not accepted Him yet. Verse 20 says in the NLT; "(20) So we are Christ's ambassadors; God is making his appeal through us. We speak for Christ when we plead, "Come back to God!"".

What then is our responsibility after we receive salvation? We no longer live for ourselves as God has taken care of us. We live the rest of our lives to help God reach those He wants to reach. How do we do that? We study The New Testament to find out how to do that.

As we observe His examples, most of us will realize that we tend not to have the "Others Centered" ethics that Jesus is teaching. In this book and others I have used the word "roll" to mean the way we do things. God always "Rolls" the "Others Centered" way. We tend to "roll" the self-centered way.

This character deficit is often the cause of altering basic New Testament scriptures or simply teaching verses out of context. We humans also tend to exhibit some of those Judiazer characteristics the Apostle Paul came against. And of course we tend to enjoy judging others rather than concentrating on our own bad ethics.

The great news is that our God knows this about us. One of the reasons He has placed God The Holy Spirit within each of us is to "Help" us to be able to be "Others Centered" like He is. It is not automatic like our salvation was. We need to continually seek God The Holy Spirit within us for His "Help".

If we do not realize this truth, we spend the rest of our earthly lives representing our Lord with our human inability. We need to have a relationship with God The Holy Spirit within us. This will enable us to tap into His power to help us "Roll" God's way.

The good news is that The Holy Spirit will "Help" us when we desire to offer the Christian Ethics our Lord demonstrated during the introduction to the "New Faith" of Christianity.

So, please don't be afraid of this relationship. And please realize that we are not who we used to be prior to receiving our Lord's gift of salvation.

Go back and reread 2nd Corinthians to make sure you understand what it means to be "born again"!

CHAPTER 8

A NEW LIFE FORM

As we wrap up this little book, I will present to you what I believe to be our biggest misunderstanding. Please go back and read the last chapter again to make sure you understand the meaning of **<u>a new life form.</u>**

1st let's take a look at a scripture that captures the difference between being "Others Centered" and being self-centered. Again, please turn in your Bible to the book of Romans 13:8-10. This was written by the Apostle Paul and will be from the NKJ. And remember the Apostle Paul was specifically chosen by Christ Jesus to be the Apostle to the Gentiles. Romans 13:8-10; "(8) Owe no one anything except to love one another, for he who loves another has fulfilled the law. (9) For the commandments, You shall not commit adultery, You shall not murder, You shall not steal, You shall not bear false witness, You shall not covet and if there is any other commandment, all are summed up in this saying, You shall love your neighbor as yourself. (10) Love does no harm to a neighbor; therefore love is the fulfillment of the law." And of course these scriptures are dealing with the "spirit" of the law.

Most believers are familiar with our Lord Jesus saying this to the young lawyer of the Pharisee's, when He was asked what is the greatest commandment, in the 23rd chapter of Matthew. I decided to use the one that the Apostle Paul used in the 13th chapter of Romans. I think it helps us to realize its importance.

Also, after reading example after example of just some of the Christian Ethics to be found in The New Testament, I think it will just naturally lead us into the final topic of this little book.

Please once again turn in your Bible to the book of Philippians 3:17-21. We will quote this out of the NLT; "(17) Dear brothers and sisters, pattern your lives after mine, and learn from those who follow our examples. (18) For I have told you often before, and I say it again with tears in my eyes, that there are many whose conduct shows they are enemies of the cross of Christ. (19) They are headed for destruction. Their god is their appetite, they brag about shameful things, and they think only about this life here on earth.

(20) But we are citizens of heaven, where the Lord Jesus Christ lives. And we are eagerly waiting for him to return as our Savior.

(21) He will take our weak mortal bodies and change them into glorious bodies like his own, using the same power with which he will bring everything under his control."

As we learned from the previous chapter, we are no longer who we used to be. When we accepted the offer of salvation from our Lord Jesus Christ, we

A New Life Form

died to who we were and were born again to who we would become. Who we become is rather spectacular.

We are now a **"new life form"**. We are part human and part Spirit. We no longer live for our selves and what this world can do for us. We live to serve the One who called us.

We understand the significance of Bible verses like 2nd Corinthians 5:17. We now realize that the verse about "citizenship" in the 3rd chapter of Philippians is about us.

The concern for the balance of our earthly lives is to be lived for one purpose. That purpose is to represent Christ Jesus for the rest of our lives on earth. They may be long or they may be short. They are about His purpose for us and not our own purpose for us.

Here is an example I would like to live by; **"nothing can happen to me that God does not allow and what He allows is for my own good"**.

I may not like what He allows. In fact, as I mentioned in a previous chapter, I have had a few discussions regarding some of those things He has already allowed in my life. I'm sure there will be more discussions until He takes me home. But that is due to my humanity and not my **"new life form"** nature.

My prayer is that I may be less contentious and more positive about this life. I do desire to be used by our God whenever He wants to use me. I also pray that I will view the rest of humanity as my place to practice the "Christian Ethics" our Lord desires that we practice. That includes all of my brothers and sisters. And never forget that includes God.

Many of you will ask the obvious question. Who are we and what are we? As I stated earlier in this chapter, we are no longer who we used to be. This can be scary for many people because they have spent a lot of time becoming who they are.

Also, what does it mean that we are a **"new life form"**? Before Jesus offered and we accepted His wonderful offer of salvation we were part of His creation of humans on the earth. Now we have died to who we once were and have been born again into a new life. What are the responsibilities of that new life? Please, study The New Testament to find that answer.

We have been given a very important job by our Lord. He has given us the opportunity to represent Him to those of His creation who have not yet accepted His fantastic offer. Also, to represent Him to those who have accepted, but do not yet understand what has happened to them.

And we must never forget that we need to represent Him as He wants to be represented and not just how we want to represent Him. As we study The New Testament, we learn His way is always "Others Centered" and never self-centered.

How is this possible? We have given up our human rights in order to serve **every** human. We know this is humanly impossible. We also know that He understands this fact. Because of this human inability He has given us God The Holy Spirit to empower us for His service.

We need to access the power, of God The Holy Spirit within us, so that we can be who Jesus wants us to be.

<u>May God bless you in this new life</u>

CHAPTER 9

CHRISTIAN ETHICS IN ACTION

The purpose of this chapter is to look at Jesus and a few of His disciples as they represented the "Christian Ethics" of The New Testament. We have a saying today that goes like this: "Walk The Talk". So enjoy a few of these stories and please feel free to look up for your selves the many examples to be found in The New Testament.

I'd like to start out with one of our favorite Apostles, Peter. Please open your Bible to Acts chapter 10. This is the story of how God lets Peter know that he, Peter, has been chosen to visit a Gentile in Caesarea named Cornelius.

In this chapter, Peter first has a rather interesting discussion with God about what he, Peter, has been asked to do. Peter obeys God after God convinces him that the "law" of the Old Testament is not part of the "New Faith" of Christianity. In fact, no longer is salvation only for the Jews. Peter goes to visit Cornelius to introduce Cornelius & his family to Jesus.

I mention this example 1st as it is one of my favorites. As we read through the Gospels, Jesus gives quite a bit of attention to Peter. We come to realize that Peter is a tad stubborn. In this chapter of Acts God chooses Peter to interact with Gentiles, which under the Old Testament was a no…no. I tend to think this decision God made to use Peter really helped the rest of the Apostles to accept God's decision to choose the Apostle Paul to be the Apostle to the Gentiles.

In Acts chapter 7 is the story of Stephen. In chapter 6 we discover that Stephen was not one of the original Apostles. He was one of the men added to the group of new believers so that the 12 Apostles could give their time to prayer and teaching the word.

Well, later we learn in Chapter 6 that Stephen gets into a debate of sorts with a Jewish group from the Synagogue and winds up being arrested with the help of slander from this group. When he is brought before the Sanhedrin, the official Jewish Council, he is asked to respond to the slanderous charges.

In chapter 7 the story of Stephen is completed. After giving an amazing explanation of the Old Testament and a great defense of the "New Faith" of Christianity, they decide to kill him. In the last several sentences of chapter 7, as Stephen is dying, we are told that he asked God to receive his spirit and ask God to not charge those who were killing him with that sin.

His courage amazes me. That he would offer the gift of forgiveness even as he was being killed, never fails to impress me. And of course we are reminded of the same situation of our Lord Jesus being crucified and praying to His Father to forgive those who were killing Him.

The Apostle Paul had many things to say about "Christian Ethics". One of my favorites is found in 2nd Corinthians in chapter 2. Many times it is overlooked because of later chapters that speak of more popular Bible knowledge.

This story has its beginning in 1st Corinthians and is about the man chosen by the local Corinthians to be one of the leaders of their new church. Unfortunately he turns out to be a bad leader. In 1st Corinthians Paul advises them to get rid of him. They follow Paul's advice and kick him out of the church.

You can pick up on this story in the 5th chapter of 1st Corinthians. Paul has been told of what was happening by friends. This 5th chapter is his written condemnation of their choice of this man. I will not quote this chapter, but please take the time to study it your-self.

In verses 1-11 of chapter 2 in 2nd Corinthians is the conclusion to this story. For some reason most of our Pastors do not teach on this. I love it because it so agrees with the "Christian Ethics" I discovered in "The Beatitudes" in Matthew's Gospel. As believers we need to realize the value of mercy and forgiveness.

For my last example I will use our Lord Jesus Himself. Please turn in your Bible to Matthew's Gospel and chapter 8. This is the famous story of Jesus offering forgiveness to a prostitute that had been caught in the act and is going to be stoned for her sin.

Of course this is the famous story of "Let him who has not sinned cast the 1st stone". The bottom line is not that she had not sinned, but the "Christian Ethics" that Jesus applies to the situation. That of course would be the principle of "Christian Ethics" in the form of mercy.

The beautiful examples I have mentioned point out the application of "Christian Ethics". These, usually, are different than the ethics human's value. I believe some of the scriptures we need to look at are found in 1st Corinthians in chapter 2 and verses 10-12. The NLT says it this way; "(10) But it was to us that God revealed these things by his Spirit. For his Spirit searches out everything and shows us God's deep secrets. (11) No one can know a person's thoughts except that persons own spirit, and no one can know God's thoughts except God's own Spirit. (12) And we have received God's Spirit (not the world's spirit), so we can know the wonderful things God has freely given us."

I believe the previous scriptures are the reason only believers can believe God's Wisdom over the world's wisdom. And remember, when there is a difference between the world's wisdom and God's Wisdom, His Wisdom is right.

Please turn in your Bible to 2nd Corinthians, chapter 3 & verses 13-18. The NLT says it this way; "(13) We are not like Moses, who put a veil over his face so the people of Israel would not see the glory even though it was destined to fade away. (14) But the people's minds were hardened, and to this day whenever the old covenant is being read, the same veil covers their minds so they cannot understand the truth. And this veil can be removed only by believing in Christ. (15) Yes, even today when they read Moses writings, their hearts are covered with that veil, and they do not understand. (16) But whenever someone turns to the Lord, the veil is taken away. (17) For the Lord is the Spirit, and wherever the Spirit of the Lord is, there is freedom. (18) So all of us who have had that veil removed can see and reflect the glory of the Lord. And the Lord—who is the Spirit—makes us more and more like him as we are changed into his glorious image".

All humans today tend to have a veil over their eyes that prevents them from seeing and believing God's Wisdom. Remember, it is "the bad dude" who is in control of this Earth today. It is only after we have believed in the gift of salvation, that our Lord Jesus offers us, that we receive The Holy Spirit within us that remove's the veil that allows us to believe in God's Wisdom.

Its not that humans, who have not received our Lord's free gift of salvation, cannot be "Others

Centered". After all, we have all been created with parts of God inherit within us. It's just that humans also have a greater tendency to be self-centered.

This is why I believe that God has given us His Holy Spirit in order that all who have accepted Him can have the ability to also be "Others Centered". As I mentioned earlier in this little book, Jesus told His disciples that He would send them God The Holy Spirit to live within them. The reasons Jesus said He would do this speaks' to the disciples need of help.

He knew that after He was crucified and returned to His Father's side in Heaven, that they would need this special help. If they needed the help of God The Holy Spirit within them, it seems obvious that we also need that help.

Again, I want to repeat how we receive that special help. It is not automatic like salvation. Just because He is within us does not mean that we automatically have the ability to be like God.

We need to consciously seek His help, day by day, so that we can be "Others Centered".

So I encourage us daily to access this help our Lord has given us when we receive His offer of salvation.

I know that my desire is to be all God wants me to be in my earthly life. After arriving at a Biblical understanding of 2nd Corinthians 5:17, I realize that with the help of the "Helper" I can be all He wants me to be.

It does not happen automatically. My human self-centeredness continually looks out for my own needs. But, it does happen day by day as I seek the help of the "Helper". Have I totally changed my self-centeredness? No, not totally.

But, I'm more "Others Centered" than I used to be. I find it interesting that our Lord allows me to see when I'm more concerned with the needs of others than my own needs.

So please, allow our Lord to help you understand why you are still alive on this earth.

I'm going to repeat that bit of personal knowledge I wrote in a previous chapter.

"Nothing can happen to us that our God does not allow and He only allows it for our good. And remember, Romans 8:28 is about His purpose and not our purpose."

CHAPTER 10

SO WHAT AM I SAYING

I know that I have asked you to walk a few miles in my shoes. I pray that my position will not seem so strange when you look at it through the eyes of New Testament scriptures I have chosen.

Perhaps the main purpose of this book was to help you understand how humans have changed the "New Faith" of Christianity to enhance their own personal position. Within this main purpose would be the problem of "Who Created Whom?"

The bottom line that I have discovered and tried to present in this little book deals with God's <u>"Others Centered"</u> style of love. And of course His desire that we, after salvation, will also desire to be more "Others Centered" and less self- centered.

The salvation He has offered and that we have accepted guarantees that when this earthly life is over we, with the help of God The Holy Spirit, will go directly to Heaven. This is a free offer. There is nothing required of us to receive this free gift. We cannot earn it with any good thing we might do. So what is that free gift?

As we discovered from reading Romans 8:28-39, it's a done deal. We, by just believing, will spend eternity with our God in Heaven. It's such a done deal that we have been given verses like 2nd Corinthians 5:17 that help us realize that we are half way there. We are no longer who we used to be prior to salvation. With the help of God The Holy Spirit within us we are now capable of developing that "Others Centered" personality that our God has.

Before allowing God The Holy Spirit to help us, we felt that it was necessary to personally defend God to others. Now we realize that our God is capable of

So What Am I Saying

defending Himself to all. With this knowledge we are free to love all people even if they will not understand what we believe.

Through the words of Jesus and His 1st disciples we have come to understand the "spirit" of the law as compared to the letter of the law. Through those great verses I mentioned earlier in this book from the Apostle Paul we know the importance of Romans 13:8-10 and their encouragement to love our neighbor.

But perhaps the most important message this little book offers is to help us realize that we are "milk toast" and "wimps". We need not defend ourselves as our God protects us when we need it. That is unless He is allowing something to happen in our lives to shape us into the image of Jesus.

!!! THAT IS A GOOD THING !!!

As I mentioned earlier in this book, it may not always feel like a good thing. But trust me, it is a good thing. The reason it is a good thing is that our free gift of salvation has already given us the greatest gift anyone could receive.

The whole world would love to have the confidence to believe that they would be selected by God to live with Him in Heaven forever. The Apostle Paul, in Ephesians 1:13-14, in the NLT says; "(13) And now you Gentiles have also heard the truth, the Good News that God saves you. And when you believed in Christ, he identified you as His own by giving you the Holy Spirit, whom he promised long ago. (14) The Spirit is God's guarantee that he will give us the inheritance he promised and that he has purchased us to be his own people. He did this so we would praise and glorify him." Not too shabby huh?

So please, allow our Lord to use you. Open up to God The Holy Spirit within you and let Him help you to "Roll" as He "Rolls".

We no longer need to be concerned with watching after our own needs. God is now in charge of that. From now on our concern is allowing God to use us as He pleases.

So What Am I Saying

So congratulations. Through God's unbelievable love, we have been offered and received His free gift of salvation. Please, freely offer Him your life in return for anything He would like to use it for.

2nd Corinthians 5:17, in the NJK states; "Therefore, if anyone is in Christ, he is a new creation; old things have passed away; behold all things have become new."

Because God has caused us to be **"a new life form"**; with the help of "The Helper", we can do anything our God desires that we do.

The problem would appear to be that we would rather be in control of our own lives. We take the forgiveness and life forever with our Lord in Heaven, but we want to be in control of this part of our lives. We tend to tell God, through our actions, to keep God The Holy Spirit from interfering in our lives.

So please allow our Lord to love and help you in this life. Those of us He has chosen are very fortunate. Never forget how much He loves you and desires for you to love all those He brings your way day by day. And as the slogan of one of my favorite sports shoe says;

!!! SO JUST DO IT !!!

CPSIA information can be obtained
at www.ICGtesting.com
Printed in the USA
FSOW04n0710280515
7471FS